Volcano-Monitoring Instrumentation in the United States, 2008

By Marianne Guffanti, Angela K. Diefenbach, John W. Ewert, David W. Ramsey, Peter F. Cervelli, and Steven P. Schilling

Open-File Report 2009–1165

U.S. Department of the Interior
U.S. Geological Survey

U.S. Department of the Interior
KEN SALAZAR, Secretary

U.S. Geological Survey
Marcia K. McNutt, Director

U.S. Geological Survey, Reston, Virginia: 2010

For more information on the USGS—the Federal source for science about the Earth, its natural and living resources, natural hazards, and the environment, visit http://www.usgs.gov or call 1-888-ASK-USGS

For an overview of USGS information products, including maps, imagery, and publications, visit http://www.usgs.gov/pubprod

To order this and other USGS information products, visit http://store.usgs.gov

Contents

Figures

Tables

Conversion Factors and Datums

Multiply	By	To obtain
	Length	
meter (m)	3.281	foot (ft)
kilometer (km)	0.6214	mile (mi)

Above "mean sea level" as used in this report refers to the elevation (on the ground) of an instrument site, relative to the average sea level datum.

Horizontal coordinate information is referenced to World Geodetic System of 1984 (WGS 84).

Volcano-Monitoring Instrumentation in the United States, 2008

By Marianne Guffanti, Angela K. Diefenbach, John W. Ewert, David W. Ramsey, Peter F. Cervelli, and Steven P. Schilling

Introduction

The United States is one of the most volcanically active countries in the world. According to the global volcanism database of the Smithsonian Institution (Simkin and Siebert, 1994, 2000; Siebert and Simkin, 2009), the United States (including its Commonwealth of the Northern Mariana Islands) is home to about 170 volcanoes that are in an eruptive phase, have erupted in historical time, or have not erupted recently but are young enough (eruptions within the past 10,000 years) to be capable of reawakening. From 1980 through 2008, 30 of these volcanoes erupted, several repeatedly (Diefenbach and others, 2009).

Volcano monitoring in the United States is carried out by the U.S. Geological Survey (USGS) Volcano Hazards Program, which operates a system of five volcano observatories—Alaska Volcano Observatory (AVO), Cascades Volcano Observatory (CVO), Hawaiian Volcano Observatory (HVO), Long Valley Observatory (LVO), and Yellowstone Volcano Observatory (YVO). The observatories issue public alerts about conditions and hazards at U.S. volcanoes in support of the USGS mandate under P.L. 93–288 (Stafford Act) to provide timely warnings of potential volcanic disasters to the affected populace and civil authorities.

To make efficient use of the Nation's scientific resources, the volcano observatories operate in partnership with universities and other governmental agencies (fig. 1) through various formal agreements. The Consortium of U.S. Volcano Observatories (CUSVO) was established in 2001 to promote scientific cooperation among the Federal, academic, and State agencies involved in observatory operations. Other groups also contribute to volcano monitoring by sponsoring long-term installation of geophysical instruments at some volcanoes for specific research projects.

This report describes a database of information about permanently installed ground-based instruments used by the U.S. volcano observatories to monitor volcanic activity (unrest and eruptions). The purposes of this Volcano-Monitoring Instrumentation Database (VMID) are to (1) document the Nation's existing, ground-based, volcano-monitoring capabilities, (2) answer queries within a geospatial framework about the nature of the instrumentation, and (3) provide a benchmark for planning future monitoring improvements.

The VMID is not an archive of the data collected by monitoring instruments, nor is it intended to keep track of whether a station is temporarily unavailable due to telemetry or equipment problems. Instead, it is a compilation of basic information about each instrument such as location, type, and sponsoring agency. Typically, instruments installed expressly for volcano monitoring are emplaced within about 20 kilometers (km) of a volcanic center; however, some more distant instruments (as far away as 100 km) can be used under certain circumstances and therefore are included in the database. Not included is information about satellite-based and airborne sensors and temporarily deployed instrument arrays, which also are used for volcano monitoring but do not lend themselves to inclusion in a geospatially organized compilation of sensor networks.

This Open-File Report is provided in two parts: (1) an Excel spreadsheet (*http://pubs.usgs.gov/of/2009/1165/*) containing the version of the Volcano-Monitoring Instrumentation Database current through 31 December 2008 and (2) this text (in Adobe PDF format), which serves as metadata for the VMID. The disclaimer for the VMID is in appendix 1 of the text. Updated versions of the VMID will be posted on the Web sites of the Consortium of U.S. Volcano Observatories (*http://www.cusvo.org/*) and the USGS Volcano Hazards Program (http://volcanoes.usgs.gov/activity/data/index.php).

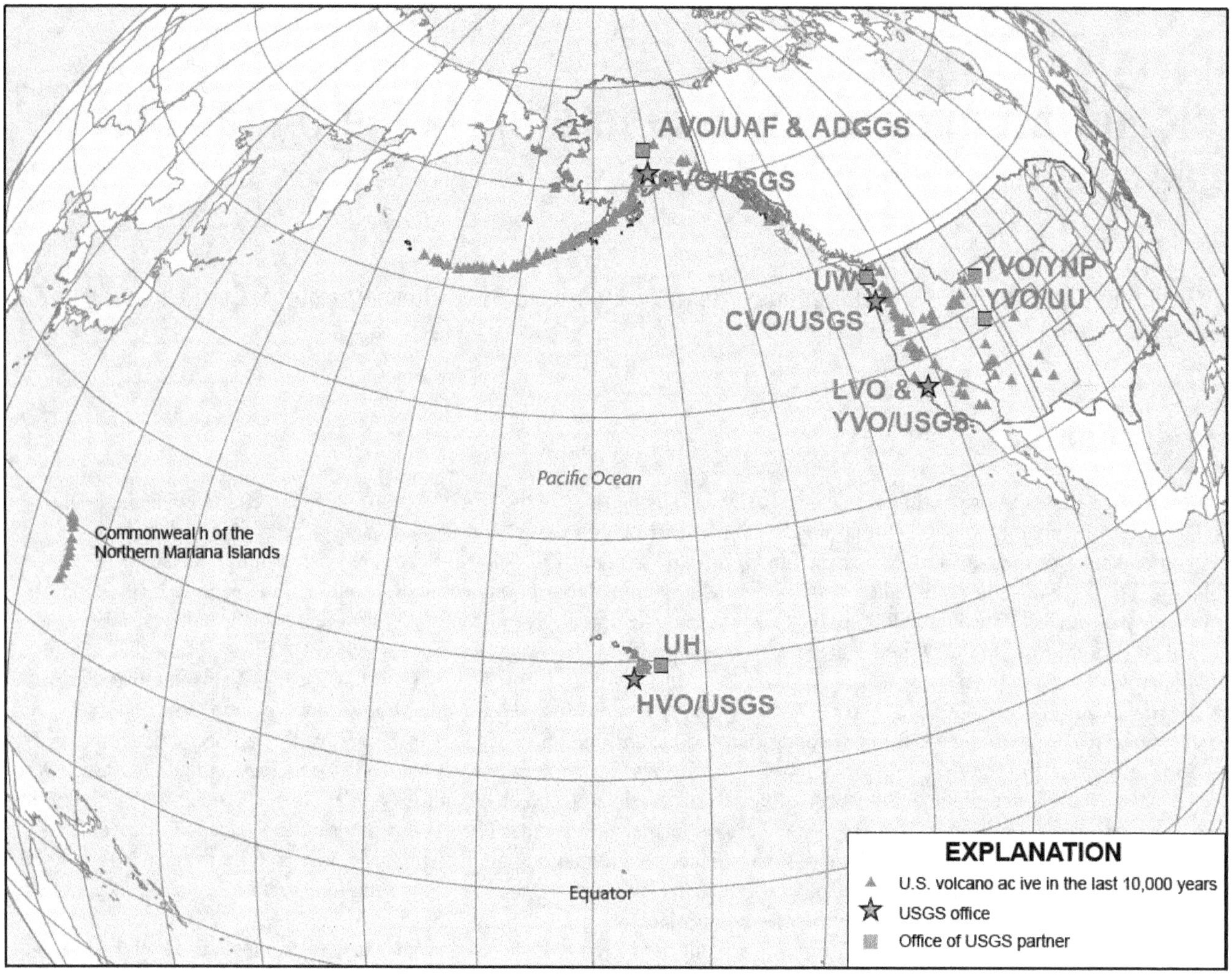

Figure 1.   U.S. volcanoes and the offices of the U.S. Geological Survey (USGS) and its partners that make up the five observatories: Alaska Volcano Observatory (AVO) operated by the USGS, University of Alaska Fairbanks (UAF), and Alaska Division of Geological and Geophysical Surveys (ADGGS); Cascades Volcano Observatory (CVO) operated by the USGS and University of Washington (UW); Yellowstone Volcano Observatory (YVO) operated by the USGS, University of Utah (UU), and Yellowstone National Park (YNP); Long Valley Observatory (LVO) operated by the USGS; and Hawaiian Volcano Observatory (HVO) operated by the USGS and the University of Hawaii (UH).

Database Fields

Each installed instrument has a unique record in the VMID. Where multiple sensors are located at a single site (as in a borehole), there are multiple entries with the same latitude, longitude, and station name but different codes for instrument types. Data about each instrument are assembled in the following fields:

SPONSOR:

Funding agency that paid for the instrument

OPERATOR:

Group that operates and maintains the instrument

VO:

U.S. volcano observatory that uses the data from the instrument

STATION:

Unique instrument identifier assigned by the operator

SITE:

Brief text description of the place where the instrument is sited

CLOSEST_VOLCANO:

Name of volcano closest to the instrument, with no set distance threshold

SI_VNUM:

Unique number assigned to the closest volcano by the Smithsonian Institution's Global Volcanism Program

INSTR_TYPE:

Instrument type; see coded lists of the various types in the following section

SENSOR:

Specific model of the instrument

LATITUDE, LONGITUDE:

Station location in decimal degrees (referenced to World Geodetic System of 1984)

ELEV:

Elevation of the instrument site above mean sea level in meters; instruments installed at depth are assigned ground surface elevation.

STATE:

Postal abbreviation for the State in which instrument is located

LAND_MGR:

Land management agency or group responsible for the land unit on which the instrument is sited

LAND_UNIT:

Name of the specific land unit on which the instrument is sited

WILDERNESS_AREA:

Check box indicating whether instrument is located within a Wilderness Area (protected Federal land designated by Congress)

TLMTRY:

Method by which the instrument signal is sent to the processing site: none = 0, analog = 1, digital = 2. If any part of the telemetry path is analog, designation is analog.

PROCESSING:

Site where data are processed

START_DATE:

When data began to be received at data center (month/day/year); sometimes, only year is available

CLOSE_DATE: When the instrument was removed or destroyed (month/day/year); not for temporary outages

ARCHIVE:

Agency where data from the instrument are archived

Table 1. Numbers and types of installed ground-based instruments used for volcano monitoring by U.S. volcano observatories as of 31 December 2008.

[Volcano observatory names: AVO, Alaska Volcano Observatory; CVO, Cascades Volcano Observatory; HVO, Hawaiian Volcano Observatory; LVO, Long Valley Observatory; YVO, Yellowstone Volcano Observatory. Other terms: CGPS, continuously recording Global Positioning System; Hydro-met, hydrological/meteorological; AFM, acoustic flow monitor; P/T, pressure or temperature. Codes and categories of instruments are defined in the text]

Observatory	Seismic: short-period Code 1-4, 7	Seismic: broad-band Code 5, 8	Seismic: acceler-ometer Code 6	Seismic: micro-bar-ometer Code 9	Deform: tiltmeter Code 11-14	Deform: CGPS Code 15, 16	Deform: borehole strain-meter Code 17	Other geo-physical Code 41-46	Geo-chemical Code 21-25	Hydro-met: stream/ lake gage Code 35	Hydro-met: AFM Code 31	Hydro-met: down-hole P/T Code 32, 33	Other hydro-met. Code 34, 36-38	Visual: camera Code 51-53	Total
AVO	193	34	1	4	12	63	0	4	0	1	0	0	1	15	328
CVO	111	16	65	1	12	77	4	3	6	38	15	0	25	11	384
HVO	55	10	27	0	21	63	4	1	15	3	0	0	21	4	224
LVO	70	8	12	0	9	61	4	13	6	6	0	18	19	0	226
YVO	43	16	12	0	6	28	5	0	4	22	0	1	19	3	159
Total	472	84	117	5	60	292	17	21	31	70	15	19	85	33	**1321**

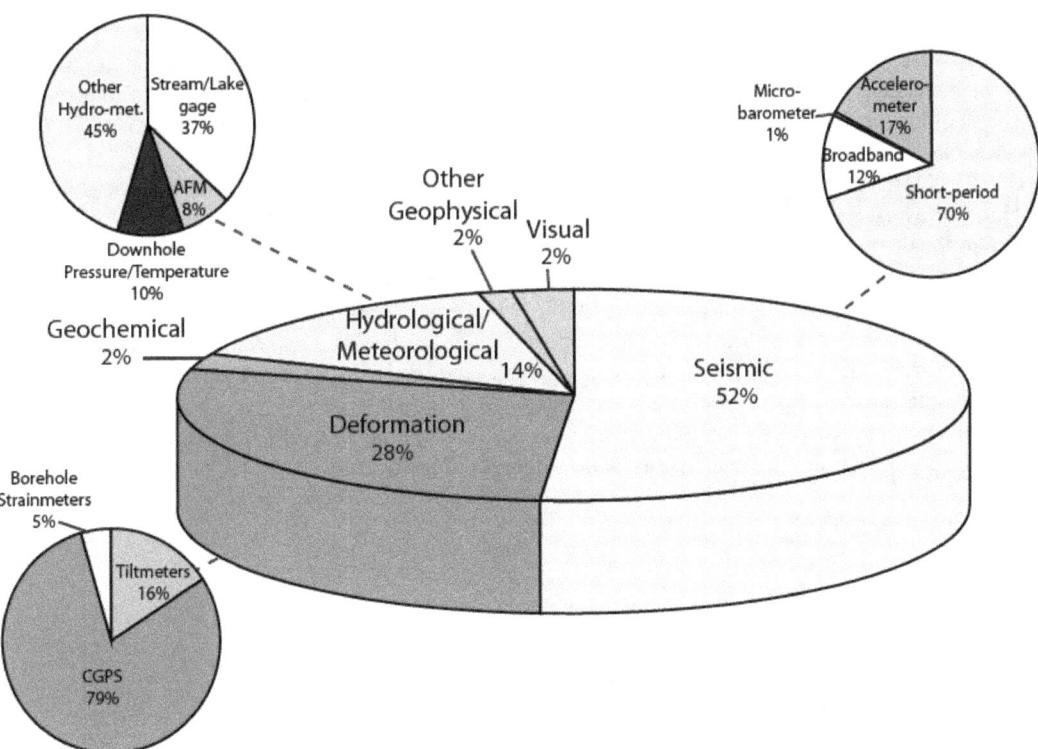

Figure 2. Pie charts showing percentages of instrument types used for volcano monitoring in the United States as of 31 December 2008. The three categories containing the most instruments (seismic, deformation, and hydrological) are subdivided by instrument type (as given in table 1).

Discussion

Types and Numbers of Instruments

Table 1 is a summary of the numbers and types of 1,321 installed instruments available for use or used by each volcano observatory as of 31 December 2008. In addition, 99 instruments have been closed out for various reasons and are no longer used, for a total of 1,420 instruments identified in the VMID through 2008. Although the closed-out instruments are included for historical completeness, henceforth in this document, the total number of instruments is considered to be 1,321.

Thirty-eight specific types of instruments comprise six broad categories: seismic, deformation, geochemical, hydrological/meteorological, other geophysical, and visual (table 1, fig. 2). In the following lists, the number associated with each instrument type is used as the code for INSTR_TYPE in the VMID; the codes are also used in table 1.

Seismic

The VMID distinguishes nine types of seismometers:

     1. Near-surface seismometer – analog short-period single-component
     2. Near-surface seismometer – analog short-period multi-component
     3. Near-surface seismometer – digital short-period single-component
     4. Near-surface seismometer – digital short-period multi-component
     5. Near-surface seismometer – digital broadband 3-component
     6. Near-surface seismometer – digital strong-motion 3-component accelerometer
     7. Borehole seismometer – short-period multi-component
     8. Borehole seismometer – broadband
     9. Surface microbarometer (infrasonic sensor)
     (10. Unassigned for future use)

Seismometers are used to track the seismicity that typically occurs before and during an eruption as magma and volcanic gases ascend toward the Earth's surface. The seismic-energy release (magnitudes), waveforms, locations, and numbers of earthquakes are the primary characteristics to be determined by monitoring. For earthquake locations, networks of four or more seismometers are needed; the shallower and smaller the earthquakes, the closer the network must be to the volcano. An overview of seismic monitoring of volcanoes is given by McNutt (2000).

Some seismic stations in the VMID are part of larger regional seismic networks that are not designed strictly for volcano monitoring. Within the Pacific Northwest Seismic Network in Washington and Oregon operated by the University of Washington, as well as at the Alaska Earthquake Information Center and the West Coast and Alaska Tsunami Warning Center in Alaska, instruments generally are designated as volcano-monitoring stations if they are within 100 km of a volcanic center.

The 678 seismic instruments listed in the VMID make up about half (52 percent) of the total number of instruments (table 1, fig. 2). About 70 percent of the seismometers are short-period instruments, which are less expensive and consume less power (an important advantage in remote areas where the power sources consist of batteries and solar panels) than digital broadband instruments. However, the disadvantage of short-period seismometers compared to broadband instruments is that the amount of ground shaking during an earthquake can exceed a short-period instrument's range; consequently, the full amplitude of a seismogram may be "clipped" during recording, rendering the data less useful for in-depth analyses.

Deformation

The VMID distinguishes seven types of instruments for deformation monitoring:

11. Borehole tiltmeter – shallow (<7 meters (m))
12. Borehole tiltmeter – deep (>7 m)
13. Platform tiltmeter
14. Other tiltmeter (for example, vault tiltmeter, long-base tiltmeter)
15. Continuously recording Global Positioning System (CGPS) sensor – dual frequency
16. CGPS sensor – single frequency
17. Borehole strainmeter
(18–20. Unassigned for future use)

Measurement of the motion (deformation) of the ground surface on a volcanic edifice is used to model the volume and depth of subsurface magmatic sources and to track the rise of magma toward the surface. Deformation is known to precede seismicity at some volcanoes and thus can provide an early indication of anomalous activity (see, for example, Wicks and others, 2002). The primary ground-based instruments for monitoring volcanic deformation are continuously recording Global Positioning System (CGPS) sensors, borehole strainmeters, and electronic tiltmeters.

Permanently installed CGPS arrays provide good temporal coverage of volcanic deformation and are the most widely used deformation-monitoring instruments at volcanoes in the United States and worldwide. CGPS data are increasingly being made available within minutes of acquisition. Electronic tiltmeters and borehole strainmeters are sensitive indicators of short-term processes and also can provided data within minutes. The optimal approach for deformation monitoring of a volcano is to use a combination of CGPS and borehole instruments together with remote-sensing techniques such as Interferometric Synthetic Aperture Radar (InSAR). Dzurisin (2007) provides a comprehensive overview of modern volcano deformation monitoring.

The VMID contains information on 369 instruments used for deformation monitoring, and they make up 28 percent of the total number of all instruments; of these, 292 (79 percent) consist of dual-frequency CGPS sensors (table 1, fig. 2). At the end of 2008, CGPS arrays of eight or more instruments were in place at 12 volcanoes (Akutan, Augustine, and Westdahl and Shishaldin combined in Alaska; Lassen volcanic center, Mount Shasta, and Long Valley Caldera in California; Kilauea and Mauna Loa in Hawaii; Mount St. Helens and Mount Rainier in Washington; and Yellowstone Caldera in Wyoming). Forty-eight shallow borehole tiltmeters are installed at eight volcanoes (Akutan, Westdahl, Shishaldin, Kilauea, Mauna Loa, Long Valley Caldera, Mount Rainier, and Mount St. Helens); only nine deep borehole tilmeters have been installed, and they are only at Mauna Loa and Kilauea in Hawaii and Yellowstone Caldera in Wyoming. Borehole strainmeters can measure very small amounts of deformation with precision but are relatively expensive to procure and install; a total of 17 have been installed at five volcanic centers (Long Valley Caldera, Mount St. Helens, Kilauea, Mauna Loa, and Yellowstone Caldera).

Geochemical

The VMID distinguishes five types of instruments for geochemical monitoring:

    21. Continuous CO_2 sensor
    22. Continuous SO_2 sensor
    23. Column SO_2 scanner
    24. Specific conductance sensor
    25. Continuous soil-CO_2 fluxmeter
    (26–30. Unassigned for future use)

In the context of the VMID, geochemical monitoring pertains to the emission of gases at the surface as a result of magma accumulating beneath or rising toward the surface of the Earth. As rising magma depressurizes, volatile components exsolve (degas) from the magma and escape through fractures and cracks in the surrounding rock. Heat from rising magma also causes subsurface water in aquifers and hydrothermal systems to boil and emit additional gases and steam. Volcanic-gas emissions are monitored for health and safety reasons in areas where the public may be affected.

A variety of satellite-based, airborne, and ground-based methods are used to monitor volcanic-gas emissions. With respect to ground-based methods, a total of 31 geochemical sensors are listed in the VMID. Continuous measurement of sulfur dioxide emission rates (SO_2 flux) can be made with an in-situ scanning instrument during daylight hours (most such instruments require sunlight to measure SO_2); at the present time, there is only one such instrument in routine use, and it is at Kilauea volcano in Hawaii. Other continuously recording stations to measure output (composition and concentration) of SO_2 and CO_2 from fumaroles and in the ambient atmosphere are installed at Kilauea and Mauna Loa volcanoes, where monitoring is done both for tracking volcanic activity and for public health and safety reasons. Continuous soil-CO_2 fluxmeters, which measure a time series of degassing through the ground at a particular site, are installed only in the Long Valley Caldera area of California.

Sampling and analysis of fluids from hot springs, crater lakes, and streams can be used to detect changes in concentration of different chemical species caused by the interaction of volcanic gases and groundwater. Continuously recording specific conductance sensors are used to monitor gross anion concentrations as a proxy for volcanic-gas input to groundwater systems at Yellowstone Caldera, Long Valley Caldera area, and several Cascade Range volcanoes.

Hydrological/Meteorological

The VMID distinguishes eight types of instruments for hydrological/meteorological monitoring:

    31. Acoustic flow monitor (AFM)
    32. Downhole pressure transducer
    33. Downhole temperature sensor
    34. Surface water temperature sensor
    35. Stream gage or lake gage
    36. Anemometer
    37. Precipitation gage
    38. Surface air temperature gage
    (39–40. Unassigned for future use)

Hydrological changes in flow rate, water levels, and chemical and thermal regimes of streams, springs, wells, fumaroles, and lakes at volcanic centers may be related to changes in volcanic activity such as magma migration and occurrence of mudflows. Continuous sampling at hydrological monitoring stations usually is accompanied by collection of complementary meteorological data (such as precipitation, air temperatures, and wind speed).

A total of 189 hydrological/meteorological instruments are located at or near 22 volcanoes; of these, 37 percent are stream or lake gages. Hydrological/meteorological monitoring stations included in the VMID are those that continuously sample and automatically transmit data, and most of them are operated by the USGS for purposes other than volcano monitoring. Intermittent sample-collection sites are not included in the VMID.

Large mudflows pose a major threat to populations living downstream from volcanoes, particularly in the Cascade Range. Acoustic flow monitor (AFM) stations provide detection of mudflows as they occur and can provide timely warning to populations downstream of headwaters draining volcanic edifices (LaHusen, 2005). The VMID contains a total of 15 AFM stations at two volcanoes (10 at Mount Rainier and 5 at Mount St. Helens).

Other Geophysical

The VMID category for "other geophysical monitoring" includes six types of instruments:

41. Gravimeter
42. Seismic spider
43. Deformation spider
44. Magnetometer
45. Radiometer
46. NEXRAD weather radar
(47–50. Unassigned for future use)

A total of 23 geophysical instruments other than the common seismic and geodetic types are used for volcano monitoring.

In this category, "spiders" deserve a special mention. These single-frequency GPS and single-component seismic instruments in lightweight containers deployable by helicopter were used for volcano monitoring during the 2004–2008 eruption of Mount St. Helens. Called "spiders" because of their spindly frames, the stations were slung by helicopter into the crater when dangerous conditions at the volcano prevented installation of conventional equipment (LaHusen and others, 2009). Between September 2004 and December 2008, 54 spiders were deployed more than two dozen times (including for recovery, repair, and redeployment to new locations). Most of the spiders were destroyed by natural events after short deployment times (days), although some spiders were successfully retrieved and redeployed. Two spiders have remained in place for years, one seismic spider functioning as a conventional analog seismometer, and one deformation spider with a CGPS, and they are the only spiders included in the instrument count of 1,321 and in table 1.

A national-scale system that can be used by volcano observatories for eruption detection and confirmation, and which is particularly useful at night or in cloudy conditions, is the Next Generation Radar (NEXRAD) system operated by the National Weather Service (*http://radar.weather.gov/*). NEXRAD units are sited and operated for meteorological monitoring and generally are not optimal for volcano monitoring owing to their physical locations and preset scanning operations. However, four stations of the NEXRAD system have been used successfully to detect and track volcanic ash clouds near volcanic sources in Alaska, Washington, and the Commonwealth of the Northern Mariana Islands (CNMI). In addition, a transportable C-band Doppler radar that can be optimized for ash-cloud detection is being tested by the USGS.

Visual

The VMID distinguishes three types of instruments for visual monitoring:

51. Telemetered camera (non-public network)
52. Non-telemetered camera
53. Telemetered camera connected to the public Internet (Webcam)

Technological improvements in digital cameras over the past decade have led to their increasing use as a volcano-monitoring tool. Digital cameras are often deployed in areas where it is not safe or convenient for people to observe volcanic activity firsthand, and they provide important visual evidence of the onset, style, and cessation of eruptive activity. Infrared cameras can provide valuable confirmation of activity in low-(visible) light conditions. The 33 cameras listed in the VMID are operated by the USGS, various other agencies, and private companies at 20 volcanoes (Akutan, Augustine, Mount Bachelor, Mount Baker, Cleveland, Fourpeaked, Mount Hood, Kilauea, Mageik, Mauna Loa, Medicine Lake Volcano, Pavlof, Peulik, Mount Rainier, Mount St. Helens, Mount Shasta, Shishaldin, Mount Spurr, Veniaminof, and Yellowstone Caldera). Of the 33 cameras, 29 are connected to the public Internet (Webcams).

Locations of Instruments

The locations of installed instruments used for volcano monitoring, as of 31 December 2008, are shown in figures 3 through 13.

In Alaska, the AVO uses 328 ground-based instruments (table 1) to monitor 33 volcanoes (figs. 3–5). The predominant instrument types are analog seismometers, CGPS, and Webcams. There are concentrations of these three instrument types at volcanoes that pose hazards to both aviation and ground communities (Akutan, Augustine, Makushin, Spurr) and (or) are research foci (Akutan, Okmok, Westdahl). The AVO has found Webcams to be very useful in monitoring the numerous active volcanoes that are distant from USGS and partner offices or other ground observers. Beginning in 1996, the AVO began to install seismic networks at volcanoes in the Aleutian Islands to help forecast and detect eruptions that produce volcanic ash clouds hazardous to aircraft flying in North Pacific air routes. By the end of 2008, the AVO had installed seismic networks at nearly two dozen Alaskan volcanoes using funding mainly from the Federal Aviation Administration (FAA).

The CVO has access to 384 ground-based instruments (table 1) to monitor volcanoes in the Cascade Range of Washington, Oregon, and northern California (figs. 6–8). As in Alaska and elsewhere, seismometers are the most common instrument, and most are short-period analog stations. CGPS sensors are deployed at seven Cascade volcanoes, with dense CGPS networks at Mount St. Helens and Mount Rainier. Other Cascade volcanoes that have a mix of a few seismic and CGPS instruments within 20 km of their reference coordinates are Mount Hood, Three Sisters volcanic center, Mount Shasta, Medicine Lake volcano, and Lassen volcanic center. Elsewhere, monitoring coverage is sparse and may consist of only a single instrument. Like the AVO, the CVO relies primarily on occasional airborne gas measurements, rather than in-situ gas sensors, to measure SO_2 and CO_2 emissions.

The HVO utilizes 224 ground-based instruments of several types to monitor five of Hawaii's large shield volcanoes (table 1, fig. 9), one of which, Kilauea, has been erupting almost continuously since 1983. The HVO makes more use of borehole tiltmeters than elsewhere because tiltmeters, owing to their high sensitivity and ease of processing, provide good early warning of the sudden intrusions of magma into the rift zones that are characteristic of Hawaiian shield volcanoes. The HVO also utilizes more in-situ gas sensors (15) than any other observatory because of the need to monitor the persistent degassing that has accompanied Kilauea's decades-long eruption.

The LVO primarily monitors the Long Valley Caldera area in east-central California and also is responsible for other volcanic centers in central and southern California and westernmost Nevada (figs. 8, 10), although none of these centers outside of the Long Valley Caldera area has shown any recent signs of volcanic unrest. Long Valley Caldera and the adjacent Mono-Inyo Craters group and Mammoth Mountain volcano have been the focus of multi-institution research efforts for the past three decades, and the area also hosts a producing geothermal field. Of the LVO's total of 226 ground-based instruments (table 1), 172 of several types are available for monitoring the unrest that has characterized the Long Valley Caldera area since 1978 (Hill, 2006). Long Valley was the first U.S. volcanic center at which strainmeters were installed, and important insights about triggering of volcanic seismicity by distant regional earthquakes resulted from the strainmeter data (see, for example, Johnston and others, 1995). Since 1998, CGPS has been used extensively there, supplementing a two-color laser-surveying method. The Long Valley Caldera area hosts the only major use of telemetered downhole pressure and temperature sensors.

The YVO monitors Yellowstone Caldera, the largest volcanic system in North America, and also has responsibility for monitoring small volcanic fields in Arizona, Colorado, Idaho, New Mexico, and Utah (figs. 11, 12), should those show any signs of unrest. Like Long Valley Caldera, Yellowstone Caldera has been the focus of long-term monitoring and geologic studies for decades. Along with instrumentation to monitor Yellowstone's high rates of seismicity and variable deformation patterns (Christiansen and others, 2007), hydrological instrumentation is used to monitor changes in the temperature and flow rate of surface waters related to the extensive subsurface hydrothermal system. Given Yellowstone Caldera's large size, the 117 ground-based instruments there (out of a total of 159 for the YVO) are sparsely distributed (fig. 11). A plan outlining volcano, hydrothermal, and earthquake monitoring needs through 2015 in the Yellowstone area has been published (Yellowstone Volcano Observatory, 2006).

The Commonwealth of the Northern Mariana Islands (CNMI) encompasses 13 volcanoes that are monitored by the USGS and the Emergency Management Office (EMO) of the CNMI government (fig. 13). At present, ground-based instrumentation is limited to seven seismic stations located on the volcanoes of Anatahan and Sarigan and on the island of Saipan, plus a NEXRAD station in Guam. Given the paucity of ground-based sensors, the USGS and the EMO must rely heavily on data from the National Oceanic and Atmospheric Administration's (NOAA's) meteorological satellites to remotely monitor volcanic activity at CNMI volcanoes, although downloading of satellite data to ground stations may take up to an hour.

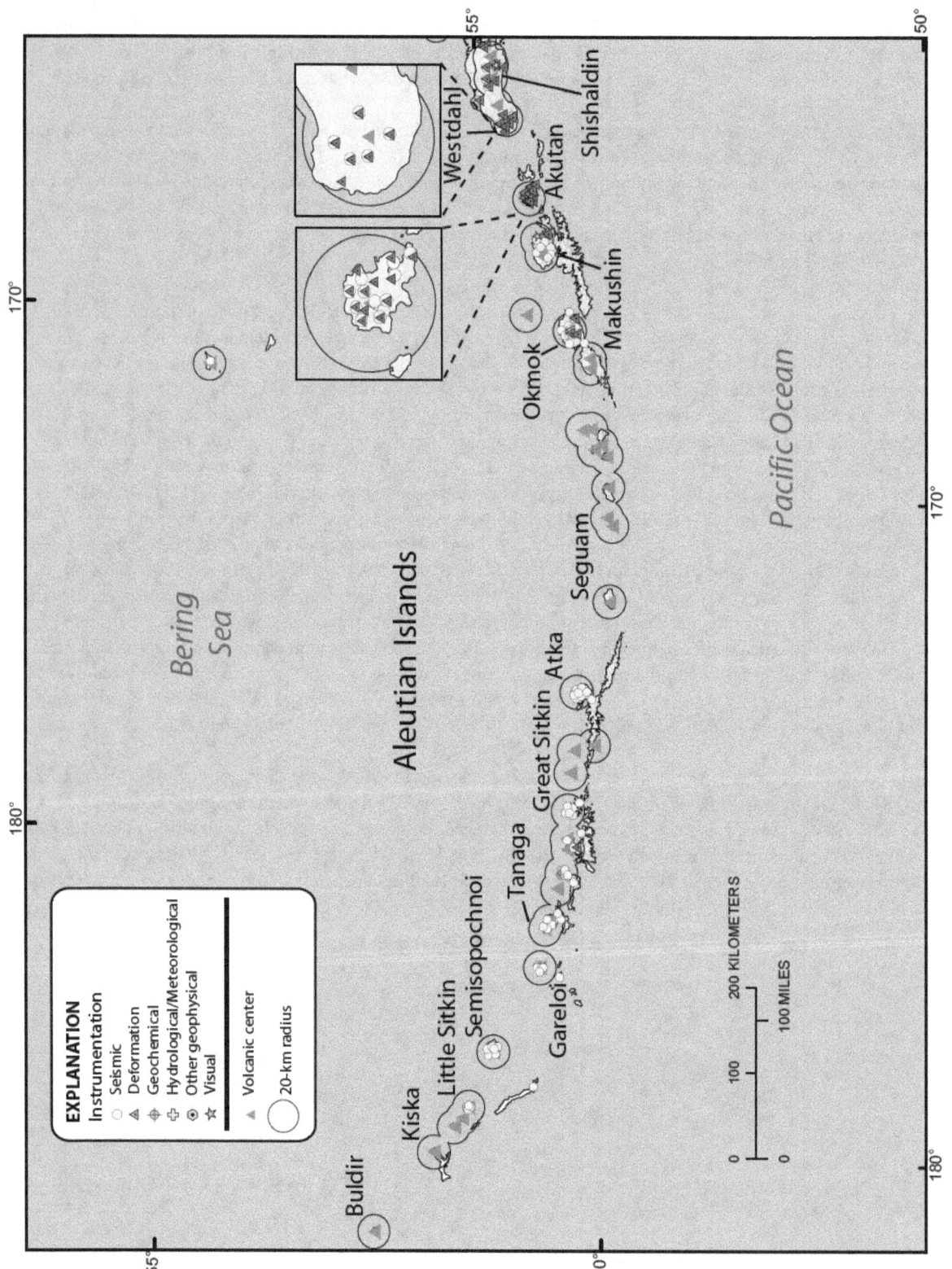

Figure 3. Locations of volcano-monitoring instruments installed at Aleutian volcanoes in Alaska. A 20-km radius is used to illustrate the monitoring coverage at each volcanic center.

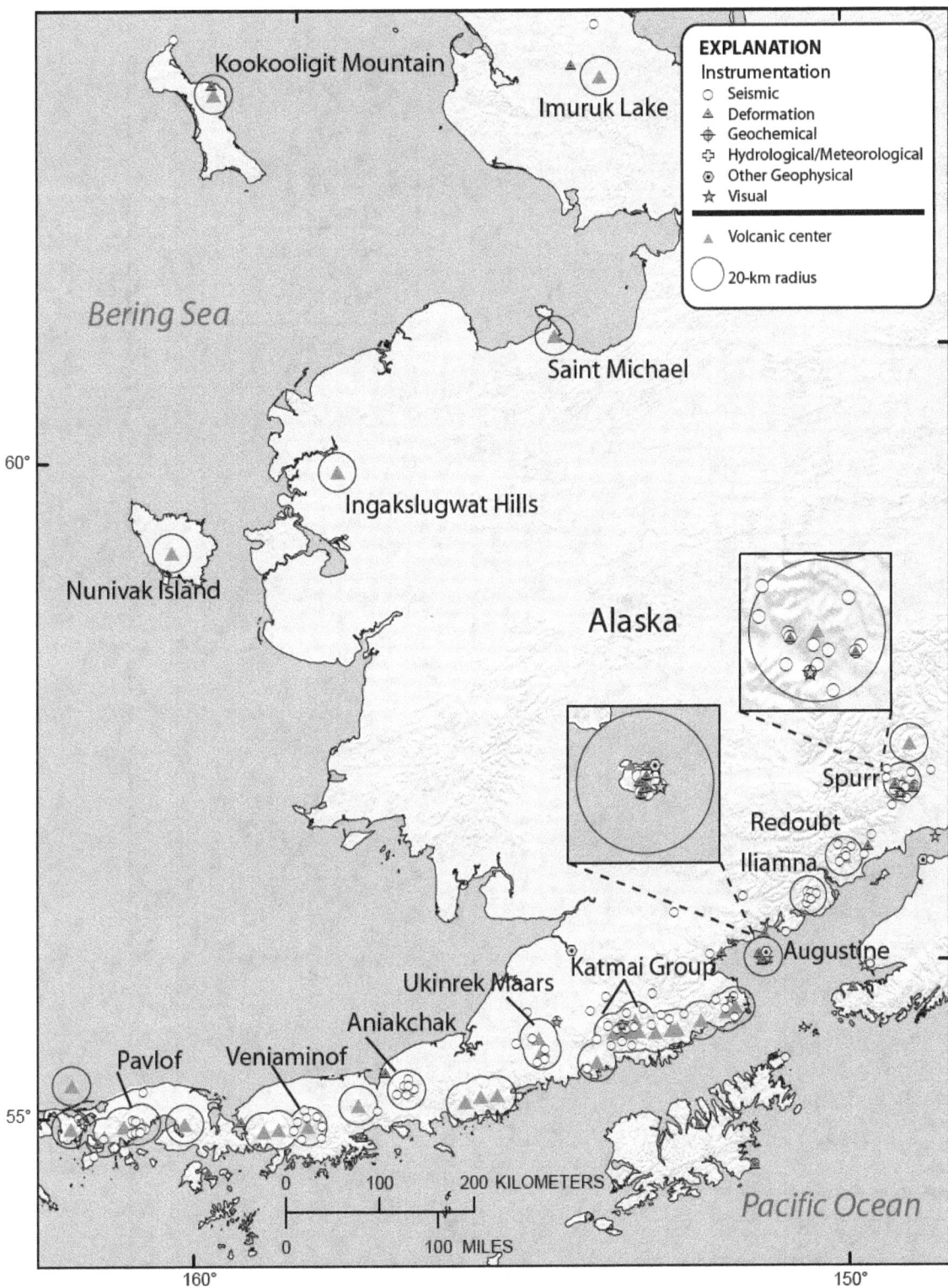

Figure 4.   Locations of volcano-monitoring instruments installed at volcanoes in Cook Inlet and the Alaska Peninsula of Alaska. A 20-km radius is used to illustrate the monitoring coverage at each volcanic center.

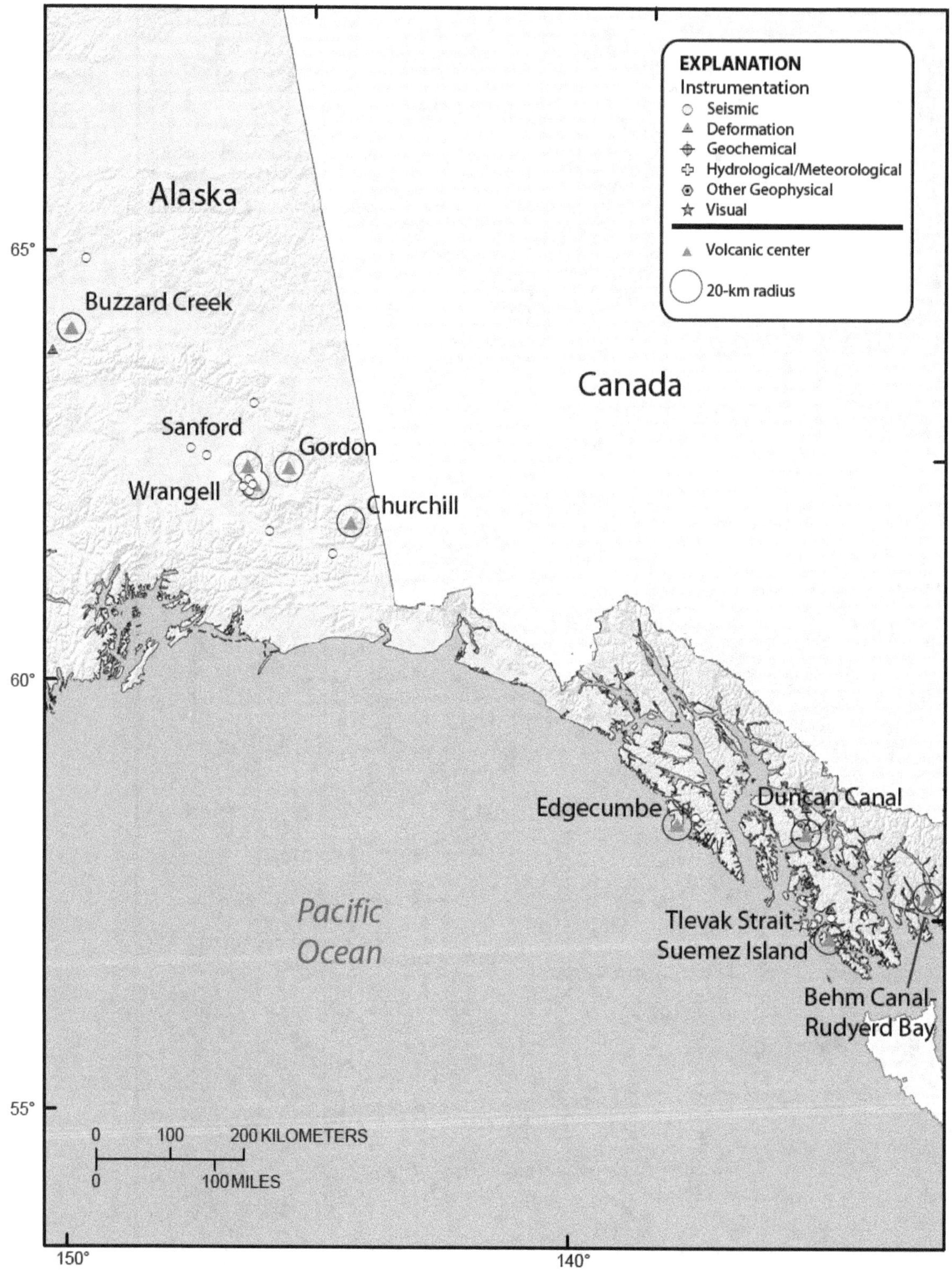

Figure 5. Locations of volcano-monitoring instruments installed at volcanoes in southern Alaska. A 20-km radius is used to illustrate the monitoring coverage at each volcanic center.

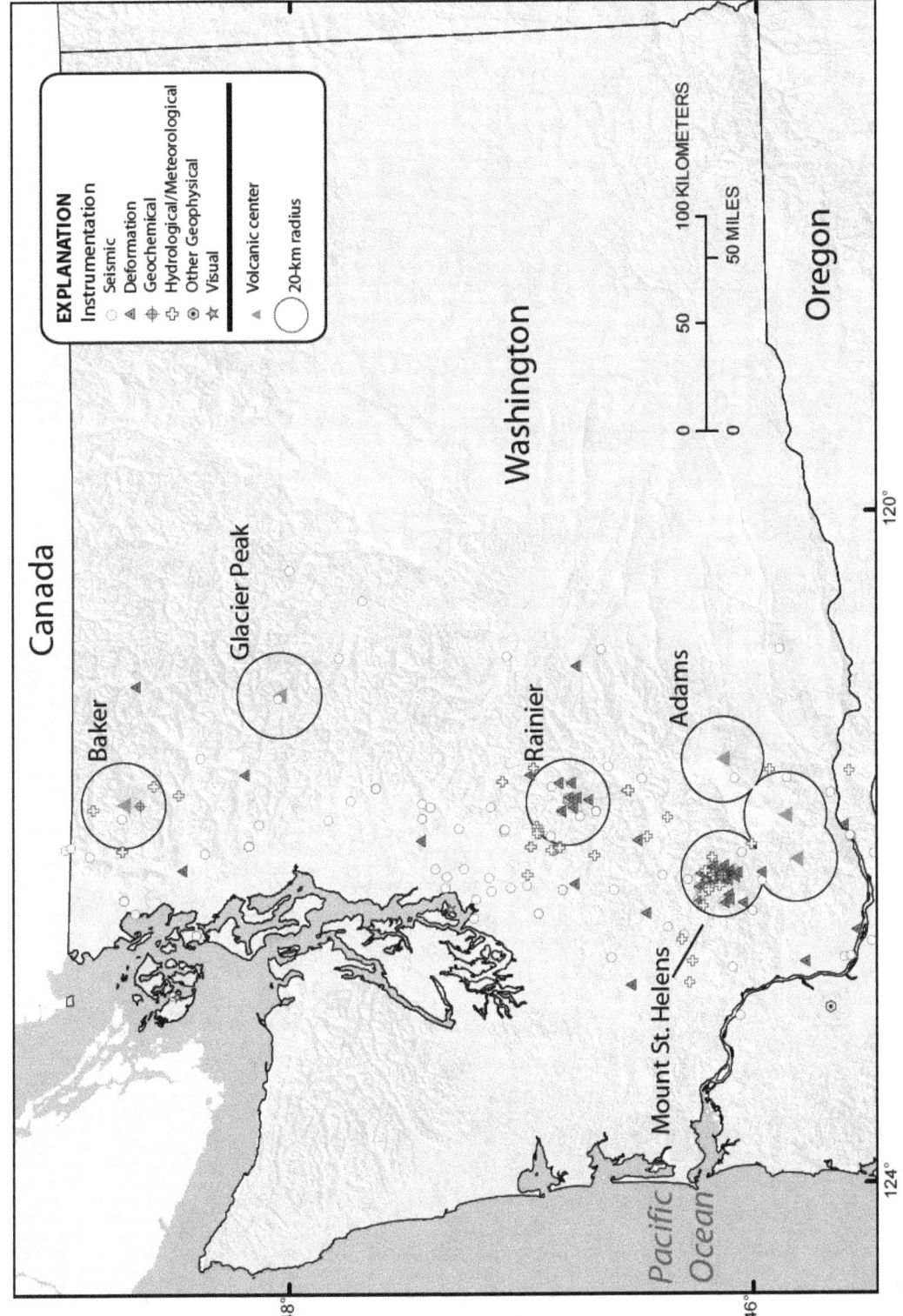

Figure 6. Locations of volcano-monitoring instruments installed at volcanoes in Washington. A 20-km radius is used to illustrate the monitoring coverage at each volcanic center.

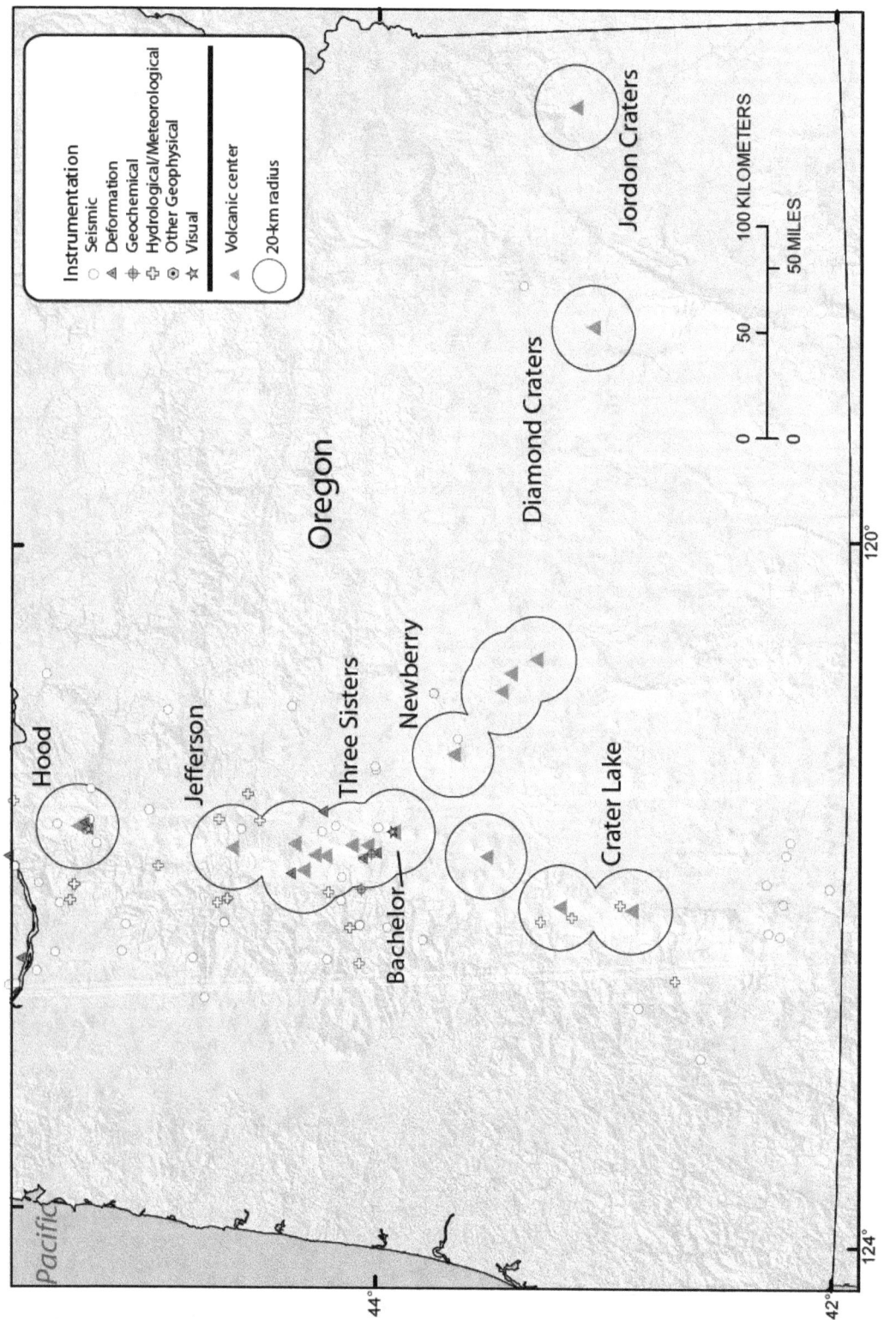

Figure 7. Locations of volcano-monitoring instruments installed at volcanoes in Oregon. A 20-km radius is used to illustrate the monitoring coverage at each volcanic center.

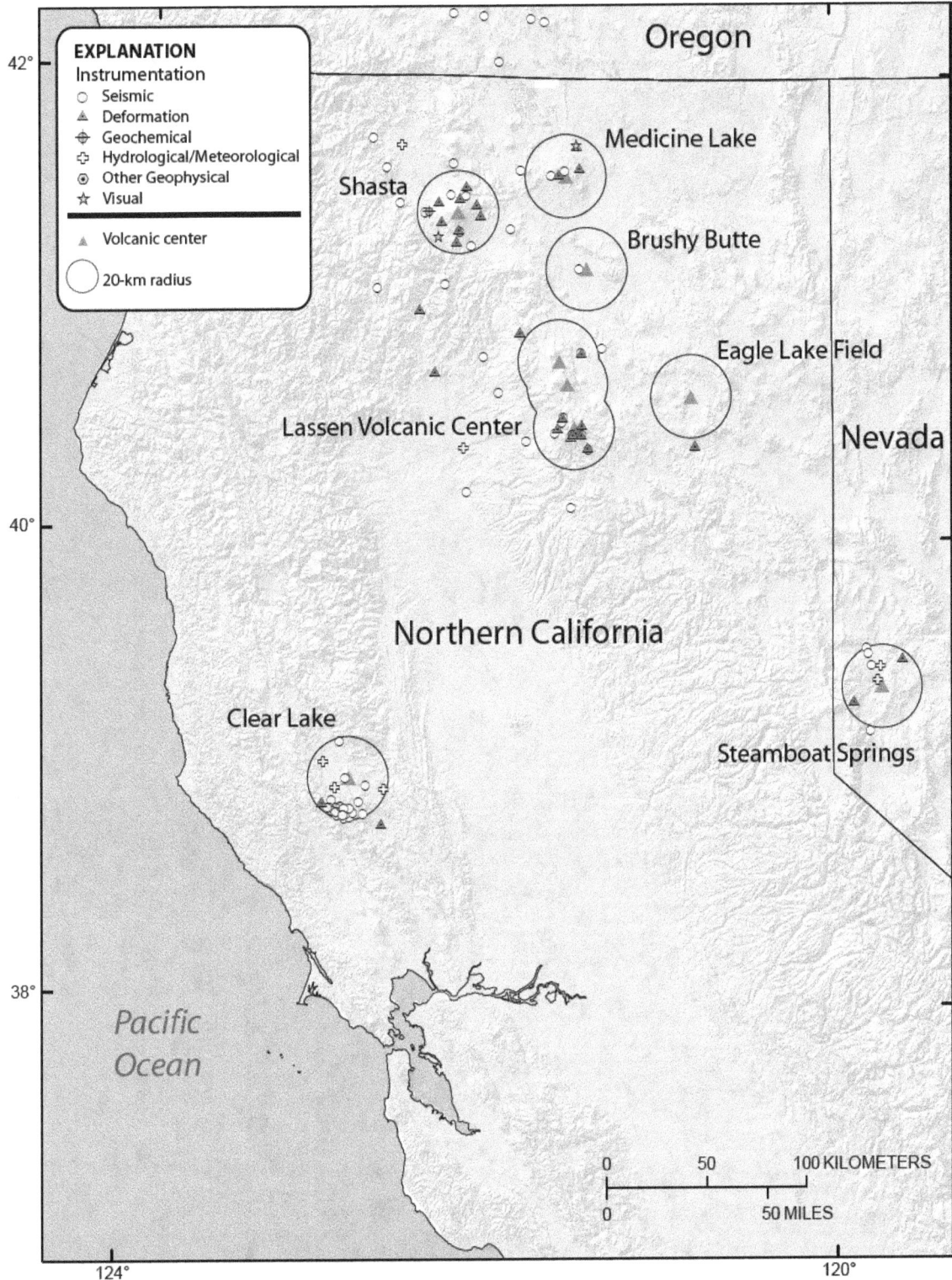

Figure 8.   Locations of volcano-monitoring instruments installed at volcanoes in northern California and westernmost Nevada. A 20-km radius is used to illustrate the monitoring coverage at each volcanic center.

Figure 9.   Locations of volcano-monitoring instruments installed at volcanoes in Hawaii.

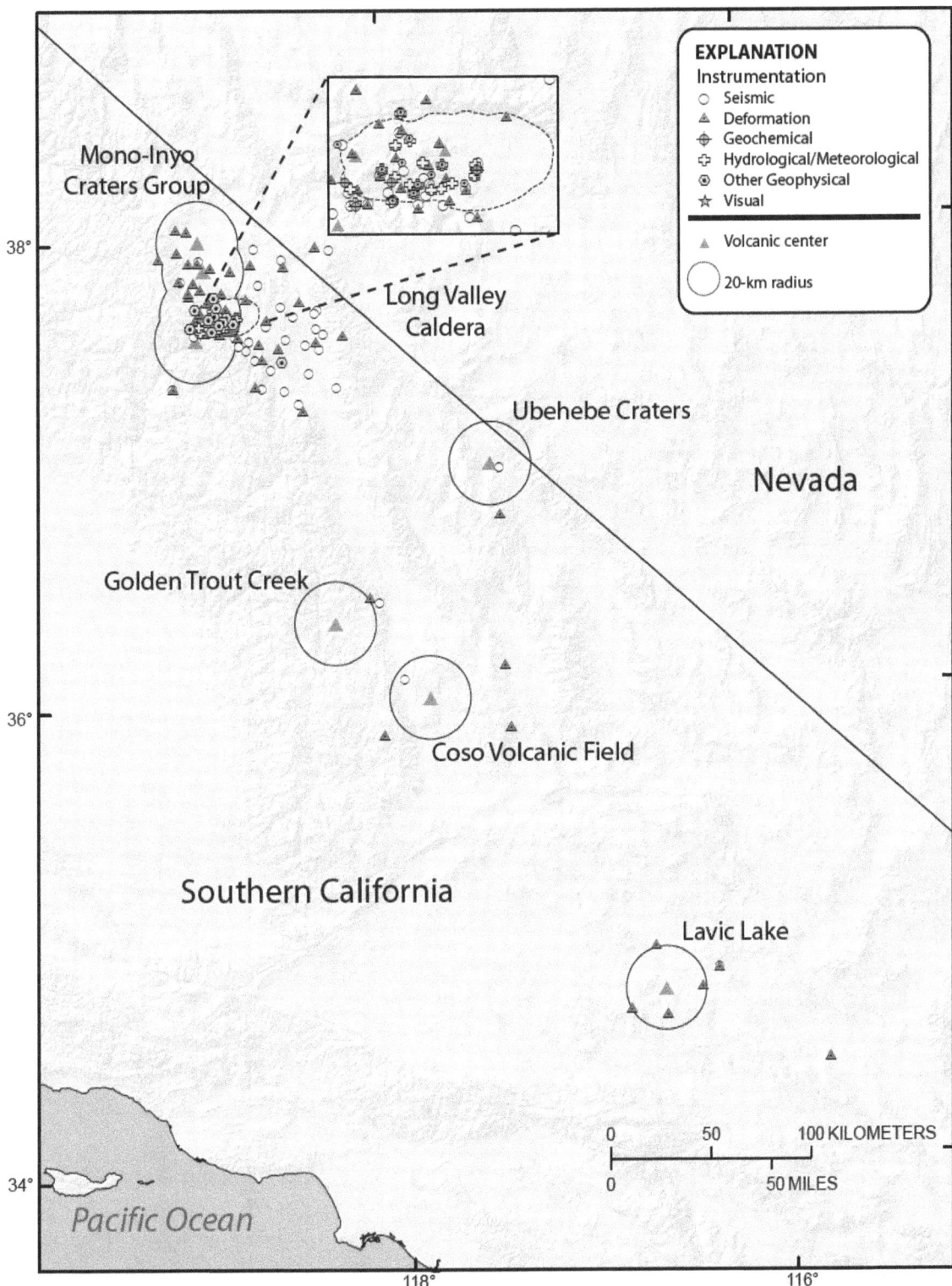

Figure 10.   Locations of volcano-monitoring instruments installed at volcanoes in central and southern California. A 20-km radius is used to illustrate the monitoring coverage at each volcanic center. Irregular dashed line in inset box is outline of Long Valley Caldera.

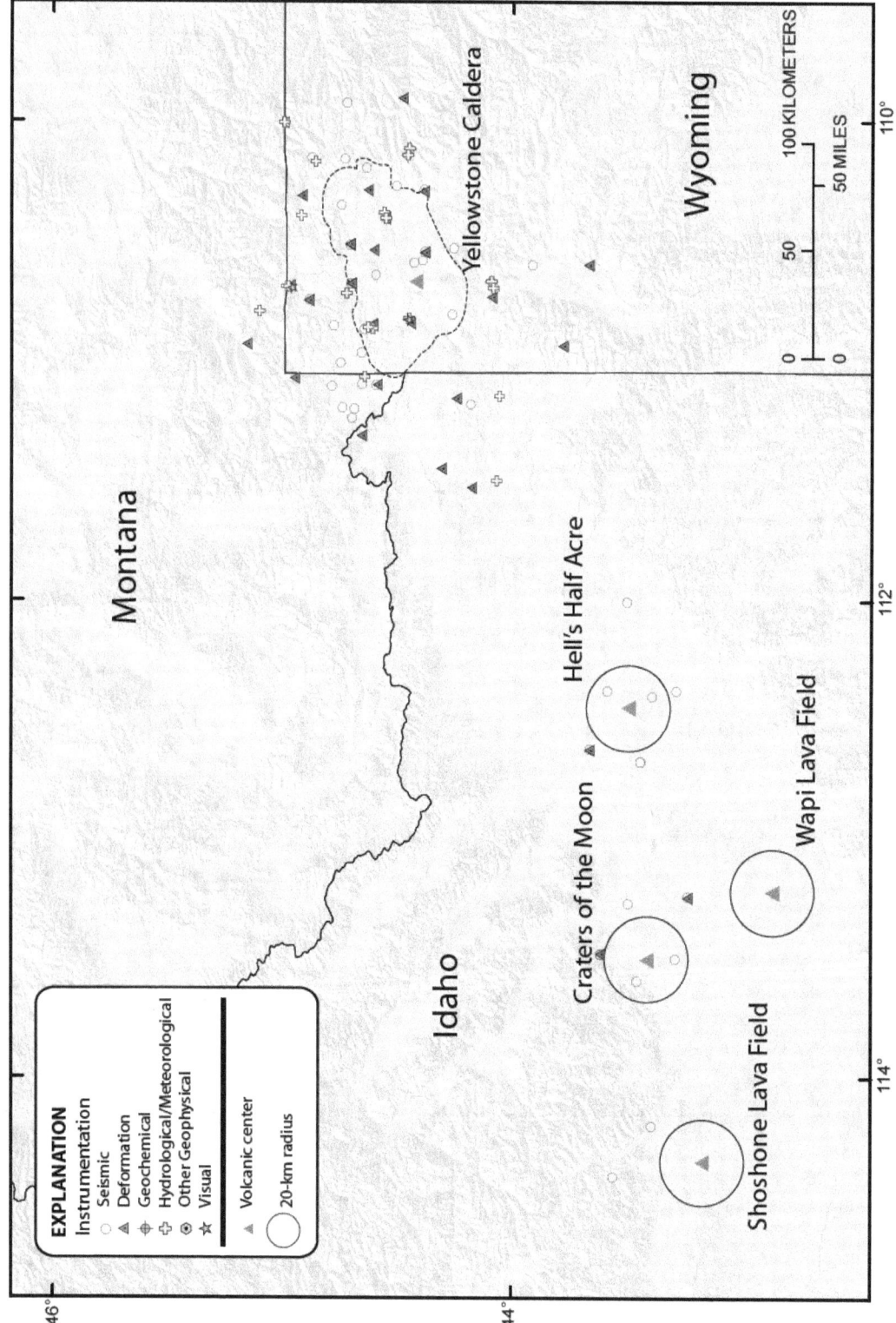

Figure 11. Locations of volcano-monitoring instruments installed at volcanoes in Wyoming, Montana, and Idaho. A 20-km radius is used to illustrate the monitoring coverage at each volcanic center. Irregular dashed line is outline of Yellowstone Caldera.

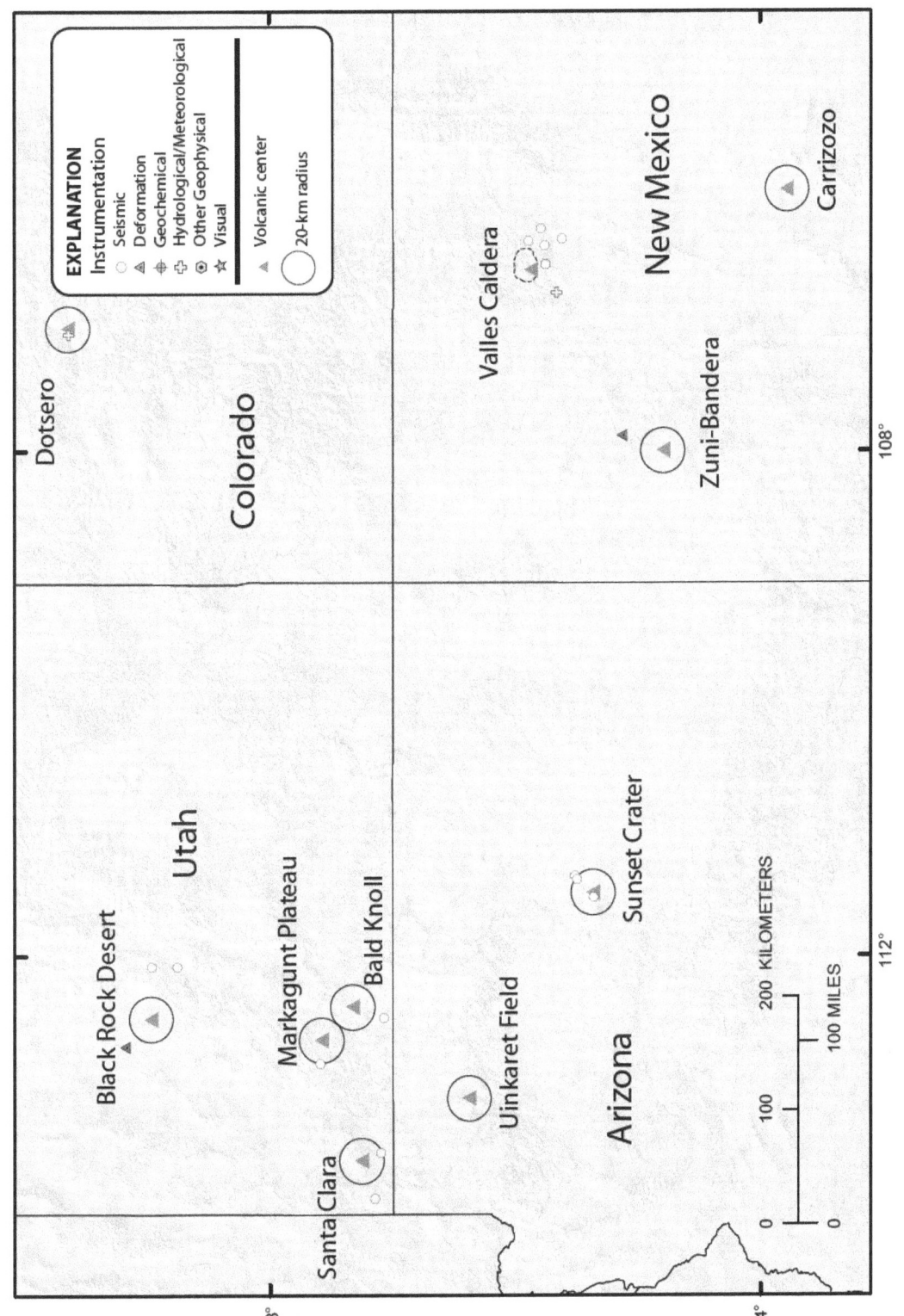

Figure 12. Locations of volcano-monitoring instruments installed at volcanoes in Utah, Colorado, Arizona, and New Mexico. A 20-km radius is used to illustrate the monitoring coverage at each volcanic center. Irregular dashed line is outline of Valles Caldera.

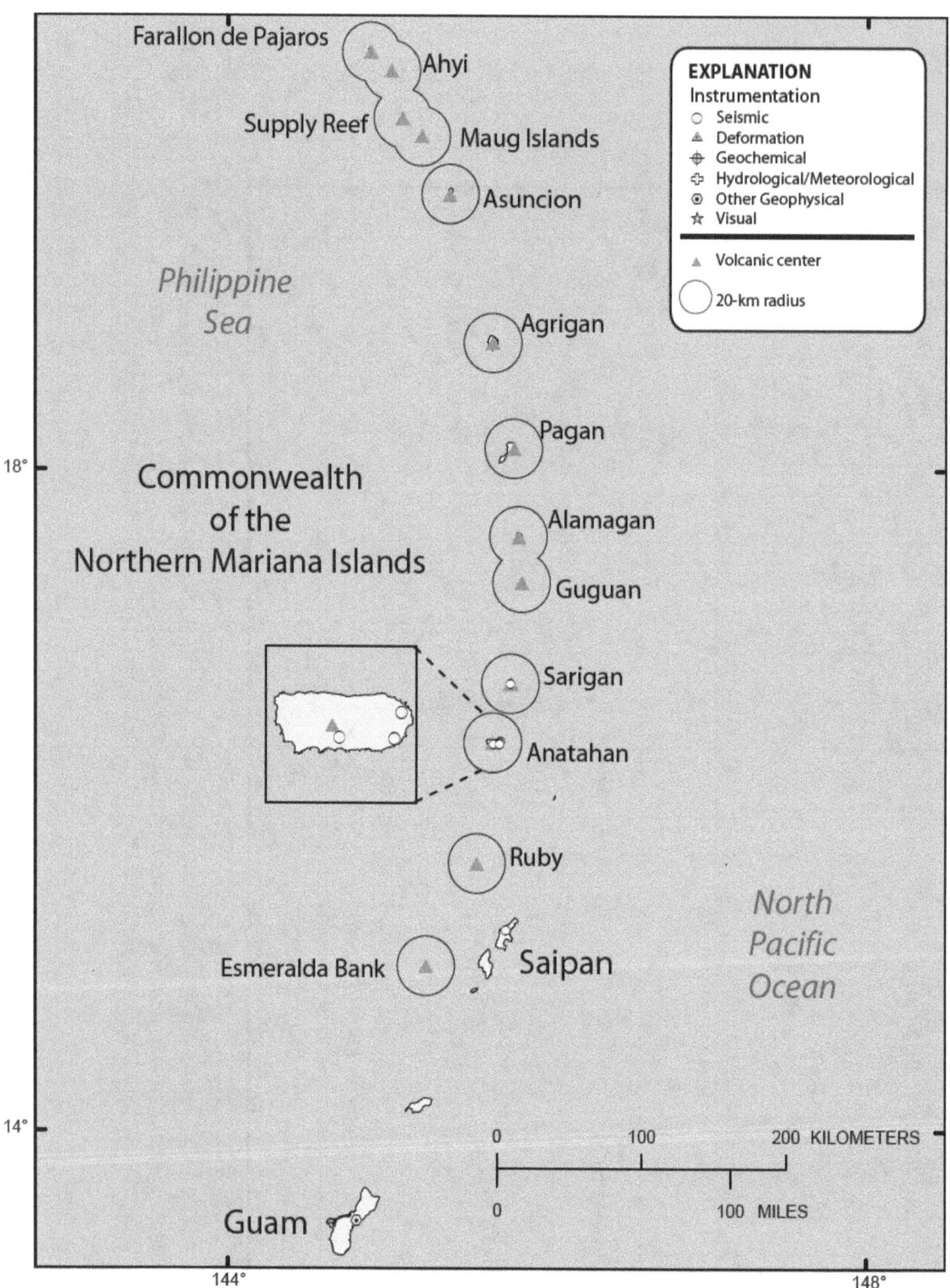

Figure 13.   Locations of volcano-monitoring instruments installed at volcanoes in the Commonwealth of the Northern Mariana Islands and Guam. A 20-km radius is used to illustrate the monitoring coverage at each volcanic center.

Sponsorship

Numerous diverse institutions have sponsored (provided funds for purchasing) instrumentation for volcano monitoring, as shown in the following list. It is common for two or more agencies to jointly sponsor an instrument. The USGS by far has sponsored, either solely or jointly, the most volcano monitoring instruments (996, 70 percent) as befits its role of operating volcano observatories. The National Science Foundation (NSF) has sponsored the second largest number (299, 21 percent). The primary role of NSF sponsorship is to support academic research that uses data collected at volcanoes. Within NSF's Earthscope Program, the Plate Boundary Observatory (PBO) is designed to study the strain field resulting from active plate-boundary deformation across the Western United States. As part of this effort, the PBO has funded arrays primarily of GPS receivers at 10 volcanoes in the United States (Akutan, Augustine, Westdahl, and Shishaldin in Alaska; Mount St. Helens in Washington; Mount Shasta, Lassen volcanic center, Medicine Lake volcano, and Long Valley Caldera in California; Yellowstone Caldera in Wyoming) in cooperation with the USGS and its university partners.

The following list defines the sponsorship acronyms used in the VMID:

*BBC = British Broadcasting Company
BSL = (University of California) Berkeley Seismological Laboratory
Calpine Inc.
Canon USA
DOE = (U.S.) Department of Energy
DOGAMI = Oregon Department of Geology and Mineral Industries
FAA = Federal Aviation Administration
IRIS = Incorporated Research Institutions for Seismology
LANL = Los Alamos National Laboratory
Mt. Bachelor Ski and Summer Resort
NASA = National Aeronautics and Space Administration
NGS = National Geodetic Survey
NOAA = National Oceanic and Atmospheric Administration
   NOAA Partnership – USGS (United States Geological Survey)
NOAA-NWS = National Oceanic and Atmospheric Administration's National Weather Service
NPS = National Park Service
NSF = National Science Foundation
   NSF Partnership – United States Geological Survey
NWIA = Northwest Interpretive Association
ODOT = Oregon Department of Transportation
PGC = Pacific Geosciences Canada
Rainier Computer Solutions
Rock Island Technology
Shasta Visions
State of Hawaii (DOH) = Department of Health
State of Utah
UAFGI = University of Alaska Fairbanks Geophysical Institute
UCSD = University of California San Diego
   UCSD Partnership – GSC (Geological Survey of Canada)
UH-PGF = University of Hawaii - Pacific GPS Facility
UHM = University of Hawaii at Manoa
USACE = United States Army Corps of Engineers
USCG = United States Coast Guard
USFS = United States Forest Service
USGS = United States Geological Survey
   USGS Partnerships – Bonneville Power Administration (OR), National Weather Service, City of Bellingham (WA), Whatcom County Public Works Department (WA), City of Tacoma (WA), Tacoma Public Utilities, Lewis County Public Utilities District (WA), Lewis County Department of Public Works (WA), Pierce County Public Works and Utilities (WA), U.S. Army Corps of Engineers, Puget Sound Energy (WA)

---

*Sponsorship that is no longer active.

Operators, Processing Sites, and Archive Sites

Operators install and maintain instruments and networks. Volcano observatories are not always the exclusive operators of the instruments that they use or that are available for monitoring. Cities, county agencies, universities, private companies, other units within the USGS, and other Federal agencies also are involved in operating instruments, often for purposes other than volcano monitoring. Forty-nine operators are identified in the VMID.

Processing sites are the facilities where data are received, automatically processed, and made available for analysis by scientists. Operators and processing sites need not be the same entities. Transmission of monitoring data (telemetry) to a processing site occurs via radios, phone lines, Internet, and (or) satellites. Most data are processed and made available within minutes via the Internet for analysis by scientists who may be located in different facilities. (The VMID documents only whether the telemetry method is analog or digital.) Forty processing sites are identified in the VMID.

Archive sites are facilities where data collected by the monitoring instruments are stored in an organized manner and made publicly available. Volcano observatories archive some data on site but also take advantage of archiving carried out by other groups, such as the Incorporated Research Institutions for Seismology (IRIS), which operates a seismic Data Management Center at the University of Washington in Seattle, and the University NAVSTAR Consortium (UNAVCO) which operates a GPS archive facility in Boulder, CO. Thirty-four archive sites are identified in the VMID.

The groups operating instruments, processing data, and (or) archiving data are listed below:

AEIC = Alaska Earthquake Information Center
ANSS = Advanced National Seismic System
AVO = Alaska Volcano Observatory
Battle Energy Alliance
BSL = (University of California) Berkeley Seismological Laboratory
CALTECH = California Institute of Technology
CORS = Continuously Operating Reference Stations (NOAA)
CSAV = Center for the Study of Active Volcanoes
CVO = Cascades Volcano Observatory
CWU = Central Washington University
Earthscope ANF = Earthscope Array Network Facility
EMO = Emergency Management Office (Commonwealth of the Northern Mariana Islands)
FAA = Federal Aviation Administration
GSC = Geological Survey of Canada
GSN = Global Seismograph Network
HVO = Hawaiian Volcano Observatory
INL = Idaho National Laboratory
IRIS = Incorporated Research Institutions for Seismology
JPL = Jet Propulsion Laboratory
LANL = Los Alamos National Laboratory
LVO = Long Valley Observatory
Mt. Baker Ski and Summer Resort
NASA = National Aeronautics and Space Administration
NCDC = National Climate Data Center
NCEDC = Northern California Earthquake Data Center
NCSN = Northern California Seismic Network
NOAA = National Oceanic and Atmospheric Administration
NOAA-NWS = National Oceanic and Atmospheric Administration's National Weather Service
NPS = National Park Service
NPS Contractor = National Park Service Contractor
PANGA = Pacific Northwest Geodetic Array
PGC = Pacific Geosciences Canada
Pierce County (Washington State)
PNSN = Pacific Northwest Seismic Network
PTWC = Pacific Tsunami Warning Center
Rainier Computer Solutions
Rock Island Technology

Shasta Visions
State of Hawaii
UAFGI = University of Alaska Fairbanks Geophysical Institute
UCB = University of California, Berkeley
UCSD = University of California, San Diego
UH-PGF = University of Hawaii-Pacific GPS Facility
UHM = University of Hawaii at Manoa
UNAVCO = University NAVSTAR Consortium, Inc.
UNR = University of Nevada Reno
UO = University of Oregon
USCG = United States Coast Guard
USFS = United States Forest Service
USGS = United States Geological Survey (including EHP – Earthquake Hazards Program, Menlo Park, CA; NSMP –
    National Strong Motion Program; NWIS – National Water Information System)
USGS-WRD = United States Geological Survey - Water Resources Division
    USGS-WRD Partnerships – Carson City (NV) Field Unit, City of Bellingham (WA), Confederated Tribes of Warm Springs
    Reservation, Portland General Electric (OR), Eugene Water and Electric Board (OR), State of Hawaii Commission on Water
    Resource Management, USACE (United States Army Corps of Engineers), City of Salem (OR)
UU = University of Utah
UW = University of Washington
    *Washington University
WCATWC = West Coast and Alaska Tsunami Warning Center
YVO = Yellowstone Volcano Observatory

---

*Group that is no longer active.

Land Managers and Land Units

U.S. volcanoes commonly are located on publicly owned and managed land such as national forests, parks, and wildlife refuges. Although permanent populations typically are sparse on such lands, temporary populations during peak recreational periods can expand tenfold or more. Moreover, hazardous volcanic phenomena can extend far downstream and downwind from the volcanic edifice, putting communities and air travelers far removed from the public lands at risk.

Most (76 percent) of volcano-monitoring instruments are located on Federal lands (table 2). Permits generally must be obtained to install instruments on publicly owned land; for sensitive Federal lands such as Wilderness Areas, permitting can be a lengthy and difficult process. Nevertheless, 191 instruments have been installed on public lands that are Wilderness Areas or managed as Wilderness Areas, primarily by the National Park Service and U.S. Fish and Wildlife Service.

The land-management agencies and specific land units referenced in the VMID are listed below:

Alaska DOTPF = Alaska Department of Transportation and Public Facilities
    Public Airport

Anacortes Parks and Recreation Department
    Mt. Erie Park

Arlington Public Schools
    Trafton Elementary School

Bellingham Public Schools
    Silver Beach Elementary School

BIA = Bureau of Indian Affairs
    Cochiti Indian Reservation
    Puyallup Indian Reservation
    Warm Springs Indian Reservation

BLM = Bureau of Land Management
    Chidago Canyon Wilderness Study Area
    Grand Canyon-Parashant National Monument
    Granite Mountain Wilderness Study Area

Table 2.   Number of instruments installed on federally managed land and in sensitive Wilderness Areas of federally managed land.

Land manager	Total number of instruments	Total number of instruments in Wilderness Areas
Dept. of Agriculture/U.S. Forest Service	408	15
Dept. of Commerce/National Oceanic and Atmospheric Administration	8	0
Dept. of Defense	6	0
Dept. of Energy/Bonneville Power Administration	11	0
Dept. of the Interior/Bureau of Indian Affairs	12	0
Dept. of the Interior/Bureau of Land Management	55	4
Dept. of the Interior/National Park Service	334	98
Dept. of the Interior/U.S. Fish and Wildlife Service	224	74
Dept. of Transportation/Federal Aviation Administration	2	0
Dept. of Veterans Affairs	1	0
U.S. Army Corps of Engineers	14	0
U.S. Postal Service	3	0
Total	**1078**	**191**

Other
Public domain land
Volcanic Tablelands Wilderness Study Area
Wheeler Ridge Wilderness Study Area

BPA = Bonneville Power Administration
Bonneville Dam

City of Bellingham
Bellingham Fire Department No. 2

CNMI = Commonwealth of the Northern Mariana Islands
CNMI Sanctuary
Emergency Management Office in Saipan

College of the Siskiyous

Colton School District
Colton High School

DLNR = Department of Land and Natural Resources
Forest Reserve
Kaena Point Natural Area
Mauna Kea State Recreation Area
Natural Area Reserve

DNR = Department of Natural Resources
Washington Division of Forestry

DOD = U.S. Department of Defense
Anderson Air Force Base, Guam
Detroit Lake Army Corps of Engineers
Nap of the Earth Army Helicopter Training Area
Naval Reservation
Upper Kipapa Military Reservation

DOE = U.S. Department of Energy
Idaho National Engineering Laboratory
Los Alamos National Laboratory

FAA = Federal Aviation Administration
    Kenai Airport
    King Salmon Airport

FS = U.S. Forest Service
    Ansel Adams Wilderness
    Badger Creek Wilderness
    Coconino National Forest
    Columbia River Gorge National Scenic Area
    Deschutes National Forest
    Dixie National Forest
    Fishlake National Forest
    Gallatin National Forest
    Gifford Pinchot National Forest
    Glacier Peak Wilderness
    Golden Trout Wilderness
    Inyo National Forest
    John Muir Wilderness
    Klamath National Forest
    Lassen National Forest
    Modoc National Forest
    Mono Basin National Forest Scenic Area
    Mount Baker National Forest
    Mount Baker Wilderness
    Mount Hood National Forest
    Mount Saint Helens National Volcanic Monument
    Santa Fe National Forest
    Sawtooth National Forest
    Shasta National Forest
    Sierra National Forest
    Snoqualmie National Forest
    Targhee National Forest
    Three Sisters Wilderness
    Toiyabe National Forest
    Tongass National Forest
    Umpqua National Forest
    Wenatchee National Forest
    Willamette National Forest
    Winema National Forest

FWS = U.S. Fish and Wildlife Service
    Alaska Maritime National Wildlife Refuge
    Alaska Peninsula National Wildlife Refuge
    Aleutian Islands Wilderness
    Aleutian Maritime National Wildlife Refuge
    Becharof National Wildlife Refuge
    Becharof Wilderness
    Coleman Fish Hatchery
    Izembek Wilderness
    Kodiak National Wildlife Refuge
    Unimak Wilderness

Green River Community College

HDOT = Hawaii Department of Transportation
    Hilo International Airport
    Lihue Public Airport

Kent School District
    Kent Junior High School

Lewis County
    Public Utilities Department

Nevada Community College

NOAA = National Oceanic and Atmospheric Administration
    Mauna Loa Observatory
    National Weather Service Data Collection Office
    Portland Airport, OR

NPS = National Park Service
    Aniakchak National Monument
    Bering Land Bridge National Preserve
    Crater Lake National Park
    Craters of the Moon National Monument
    Death Valley National Park
    Grand Teton National Park
    Haleakala National Park
    HAVO Kahuku Unit
    Hawaii Volcanoes National Park
    Hawaii Volcanoes Wilderness
    Hell's Half Acre National Natural Landmark
    John D. Rockefeller Jr. Memorial Parkway
    Kalaupapa National Historical Park
    Katmai Wilderness
    Lake Clark National Park
    Lake Clark Wilderness
    Lassen Volcanic National Park
    Lava Beds National Monument
    Mount Rainier Wilderness
    Stephen Mather Wilderness
    Wrangell-Saint Elias Wilderness
    Yellowstone National Park

Pierce County
    East Precinct
    Firing Range
    Mountain Detachment

Private
    B Bar Ranch
    Bank of Hawaii
    California Institute of Man In Nature
    Cove Ranch
    Highline Country Club
    Hyatt Hotels and Resorts
    Jones Ranch
    Mac Farms of Hawaii, Inc.
    Ocean View Estates
    Private land owner
    Rainier Computer Solutions
    Rock Island Inc.
    Shasta Visions
    Sierra Pacific Power Company
    Tacoma Power
    University of Oregon
    Waikoloa Beach Hotel
    Weyerhaeuser

Puyallup School District

Renton School District
    Benson Hill Elementary School

Snoqualmie Valley Public Schools
    Two Rivers School

State of Hawaii
    Honokaa Police Station
    Kahului Fire Station
    Kailua-Kona Fire Station
    Kapaau Police Station
    Kau Hospital
    Kona Community Hospital
    Lahaina Fire Station
    Mauna Kea Forest Reserve
    Pahoa Fire Station
    UH Agricultural Station
    Waimea Fire Station

Sumner School District
    Sumner High School

UDOT = Utah Department of Transportation
    IT Radio Shop

University of Hawaii
    Hilo Campus

University of Nevada

University of Puget Sound

University of Washington
    Friday Harbor Laboratories

USACE = U.S. Army Corp of Engineers
    Bonneville Dam
    Mud Mountain Dam
    Toutle River Dam

USDA = U.S. Department of Agriculture
    Research laboratory

USDVA = U.S. Department of Veterans Affairs
    Reno VA Medical Center

USPS = U.S. Postal Service
    Honaunau Post Office
    Laupahoehoe Post Office
    Mountain View Post Office

Vancouver School District
    Hudson Bay High School

Changes in Instrumentation with Time

The growth trend in volcano-monitoring instrumentation (number of instruments installed each year) since 1970 is shown in figure 14. There have been notable increases, most of which correspond with eruptive or unrest events, including those in the following years: 1980, related to the response to the eruption of Mount St. Helens; 1983, related to increased seismic unrest at Long Valley Caldera; 1996–1999, related to the peak of the effort to expand volcano monitoring in Alaska; and 2004–2008, related to the eruptions of Mount St. Helens and Augustine and PBO research installations. The highest number of installations in one year, 123 in 2006, primarily reflects the combined effect of the USGS response to the eruption of Augustine Volcano in Alaska and PBO projects at several volcanoes.

The optimal approach to volcano monitoring is to have instruments in place *before* unrest begins so that scientists have enough data on which to base forecasts of likely eruptive activity and communities have enough time to prepare for hazardous events. Currently, however, many volcanoes in the United States are not adequately monitored in advance of unrest to permit the best possible analysis and forecasts to be made (Ewert and others, 2005). Where this is the case, tremendous effort is required to install instruments as unrest or eruptive activity begins.

The reawakening of Mount St. Helens in 2004 is illustrative of this point. Figure 15 shows the monitoring network that was in place just prior to the onset of unrest in 2004 compared to the monitoring network at the end of 2008. In 2004, many stations had been in place since the early 1980s, and although the established monitoring was sufficient to detect the onset of the unrest, it proved inadequate to record and monitor the intense seismicity of the developing situation (McChesney and others, 2009). Furthermore, the rapid escalation of unrest during the first week of the activity quickly created a situation where it was too dangerous to deploy additional instruments where they were needed (Moran and others, 2009). As the seismic crisis progressed, the limited dynamic range of the short-period analog stations was frequently exceeded at seismometers in the crater and on the flanks, resulting in lost information about seismic energy, spectral content, and event similarity. In addition, the absence of broadband three-component instruments in the crater meant that information was lost about the presence or absence of very-low-frequency signals and about source mechanisms for all types of events. Thus, not only was ongoing analysis of the hazard situation compromised, so too was subsequent scientific analysis that might have proven useful during future crises at Mount St. Helens and elsewhere.

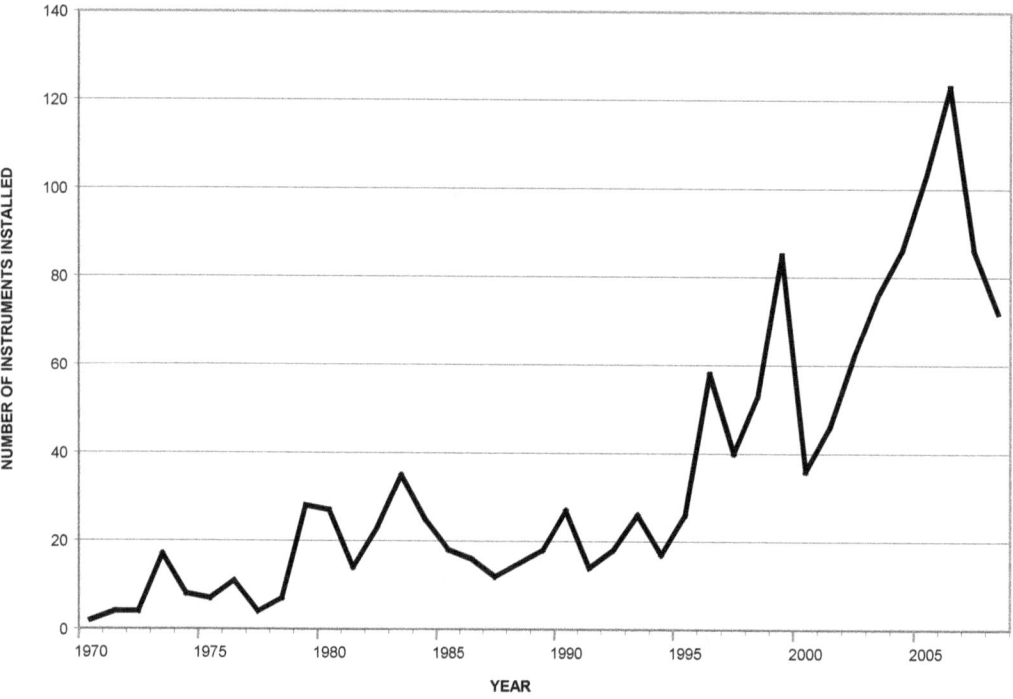

Figure 14.   Graph of number of volcano-monitoring instruments installed annually since 1970.

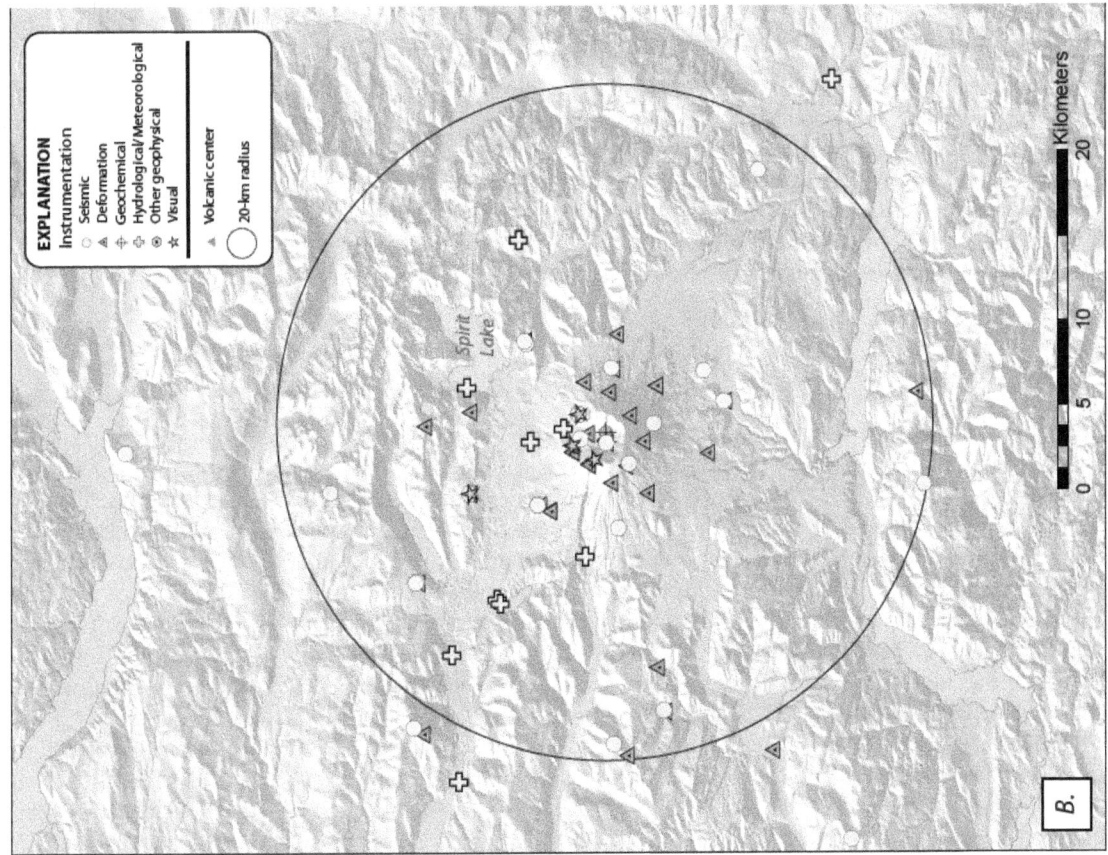

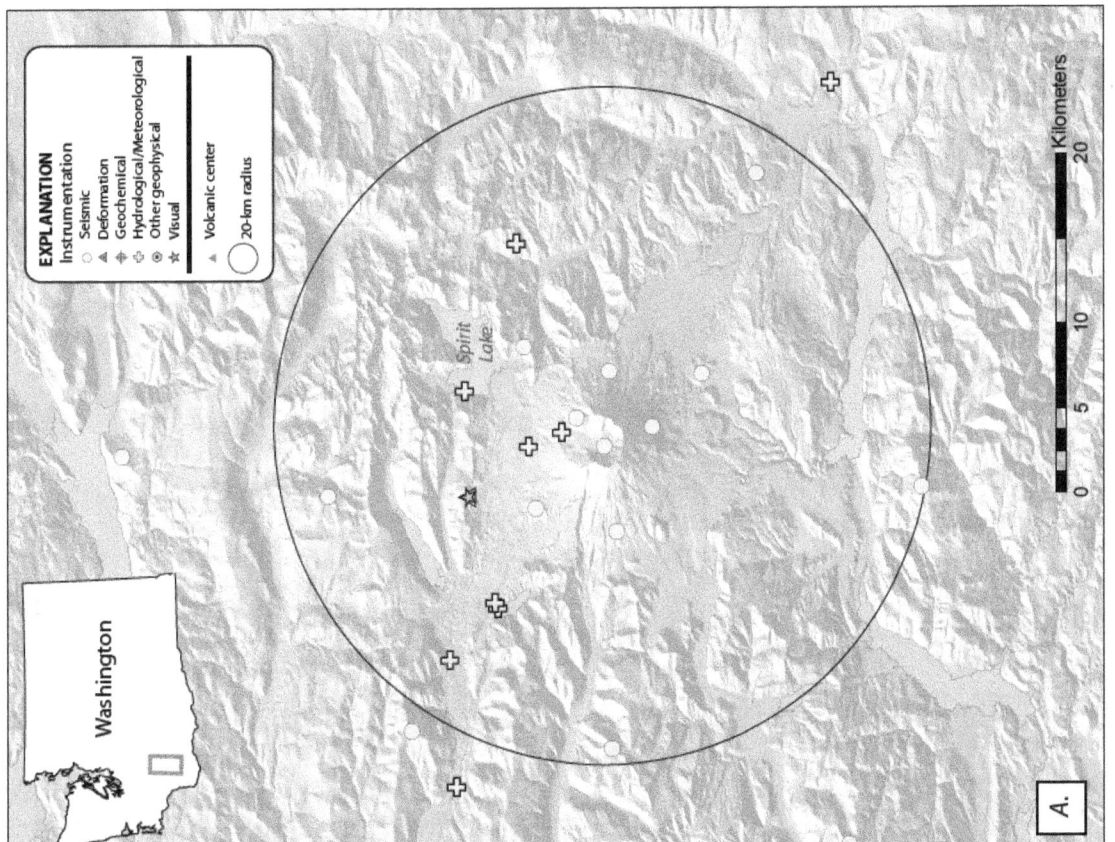

Figure 15.   Locations and types of volcano-monitoring instrumentation at Mount St. Helens (*A*) when the 2004 eruption started and (*B*) at the end of 2008. More than 60 instruments were installed at Mount St. Helens in response to the renewed eruption in 2004, and more than 60 GPS spiders, seismic spiders, and cameras (not included in the VMID) were temporarily deployed and were used for monitoring during the course of the 2004–2008 eruption.

National Volcano Early Warning System

Researching and assembling the VMID grew out of a need by the USGS Volcano Hazards Program to document the scientific infrastructure that is in place and upon which a National Volcano Early Warning System (NVEWS; Ewert and others, 2005) could be built. Apparent in this report and the accompanying database is the extensive nature of the Nation's volcano-monitoring infrastructure. However, the NVEWS assessment (Ewert and others, 2005) showed that many hazardous U.S. volcanoes remain substantially under-monitored. To meet the standards established by Moran and others (2008) for achieving the NVEWS objective of monitoring U.S. volcanoes at levels commensurate with the threats posed to ground-based communities and aviation, the number of installed instruments would have to be substantially increased.

Conclusions

The information in the VMID bears on some fundamental points about the state of volcano monitoring in the United States:
- Volcano monitoring involves many types of ground-based instruments, with seismometers and continuous GPS sensors being the prevalent types. The U.S. volcano observatories have many partners, both formal and informal, and make good use of instruments and data streams regardless of their sponsorship or original purpose. As emphasized by Ewert and Schneider (2007), the challenge facing volcano observatories in the 21st century is to assimilate data available from multiple institutional sources as quickly and efficiently as possible and to provide a cogent hazard synthesis in the form of timely forecasts and alerts that are useful to communities on the ground and to aviation. Use of data streams collected by groups other than observatories requires increasing Internet connectivity and bandwidth, in-house or readily accessible archives, good communications with the sensor subject-matter experts, and broad in-house scientific and technical expertise.
- By the end of 2008, more than 1,300 ground-based instruments were available for use in volcano monitoring by the five U.S. volcano observatories. Nevertheless, significant monitoring gaps continue to exist at some of the Nation's most threatening volcanoes (Ewert and others, 2005). The VMID, in conjunction with the instrumentation recommendations made by Moran and others (2008), is the starting point to determine the necessary improvements to U.S. volcano monitoring.

References Cited

Christiansen, R.L., Lowenstern, J.B., Smith, R.B., Heasler, Henry, Morgan, L.A., Nathenson, Manuel, Mastin, L.G., Muffler, L.J.P., and Robinson, J.E., 2007, Preliminary assessment of volcanic and hydrothermal hazards in Yellowstone National Park and vicinity: U.S. Geological Survey Open-File Report 2007–1071, 94 p., available online at *http://pubs.usgs.gov/of/2007/1071/*.

Diefenbach, A.K., Guffanti, Marianne, and Ewert, J.W., 2009, Chronology and references of volcanic eruptions and selected unrest in the United States, 1980–2008: U.S. Geological Survey Open-File Report 2009–1118, 85 p., available online at *http://pubs.usgs.gov/of/2009/1118/*.

Dzurisin, D., 2007, Volcano deformation—Geodetic monitoring techniques: Chichester, UK, Springer-Praxis Publishing Ltd., 441 p.

Ewert, J.W., Guffanti, Marianne, and Murray, T.L., 2005, An assessment of volcanic threat and monitoring capabilities in the United States—Framework for a National Volcano Early Warning System (NVEWS): U.S. Geological Survey Open-File Report 2005–1164, version 1.1, 62 p., available online at *http://pubs.usgs.gov/of/2005/1164/*.

Ewert, J.W., and Schneider, D.J., 2007, Volcano observatories and volcano hazards mitigation in the information age [abs.]: Cities on Volcanoes 5, Conference, Shimabara, Japan, November 19–23, 2007, Abstracts Volume, abstract 12–O–01, p. 61–62, available online at *http://www.eri.u-tokyo.ac.jp/nakada/cov5_hp/documents/abstract_e.pdf/*.

Hill, D.P., 2006, Unrest in Long Valley Caldera, California, 1978–2004: Geological Society, London, Special Publications, v. 269, p. 1–24, doi:10.1144/GSL.SP.2006.269.01.02.

Johnston, M.J.S., Hill, D.P., Linde, A.T., Langbein, J., and Bilham, R., 1995, Transient deformation during triggered seismicity from the 28 June 1992 Mw = 7.3 Landers earthquake at Long Valley volcanic caldera, California: Bulletin of the Seismological Society of America, v. 85, no. 3, p. 787–795.

LaHusen, R.G., 2005, Debris-flow instrumentation, *in* Jakob, Matthias, and Hungr, Oldrich, eds., Debris-flow hazards and related phenomena: Berlin, Springer, p. 291–304.

LaHusen, R.G., Swinford, K.J., Logan, Matthew, and Lisowski, Michael, 2009, Instrumentation in remote and dangerous settings–Examples using data from GPS "spider" deployments during the 2004–2005 eruption of Mount St. Helens, Washington, chap. 16 *of* Sherrod, D.R., Scott, W.E., and Stauffer, P.H., eds., A volcano rekindled—The renewed eruption of Mount St. Helens, 2004–2006: U.S. Geological Survey Professional Paper 1750, p. 335–345, available online at *http://pubs.usgs.gov/pp/1750/.*

McChesney, P.J., Couchman, M.R., Moran, S.C., Lockhart, A.B., Swinford, K.J., and LaHusen, R.G., 2009, Seismic-monitoring changes and the remote deployment of seismic stations (seismic spider) at Mount St. Helens, 2004–2005, chap. 7 *of* Sherrod, D.R., Scott, W.E., and Stauffer, P.H., eds., A volcano rekindled—The renewed eruption of Mount St. Helens, 2004–2006: U.S. Geological Survey Professional Paper 1750, p. 129–140, available online at *http://pubs.usgs.gov/pp/1750/.*

McNutt, S.R., 2000, Seismic monitoring, *in* Sigurdsson, Haraldur, and others, eds., Encyclopedia of volcanoes: San Diego, Academic Press, p. 1015–1033.

Moran, S.C., Freymueller, J.T., LaHusen, R.G., McGee, K.A., Poland, M.P., Power, J.A., Schmidt, D.A., Schneider, D.J., Stephens, George, Werner, C.A., and White, R.A., 2008, Instrumentation recommendations for volcano monitoring at U.S. volcanoes under the National Volcano Early Warning System: U.S. Geological Survey Scientific Investigations Report 2008–5114, 47 p., available online at *http://pubs.usgs.gov/sir/2008/5114/.*

Moran, S.C., McChesney, P.J., and Lockhart, A.B., 2009, Seismicity and infrasound associated with explosions at Mount St. Helens, 2004–2005, chap. 6 *of* Sherrod, D.R., Scott, W.E., and Stauffer, P.H., eds., A volcano rekindled—The renewed eruption of Mount St. Helens, 2004–2006: U.S. Geological Survey Professional Paper 1750, p. 111–127, available online at *http://pubs.usgs.gov/pp/1750/.*

Siebert, Lee, and Simkin, Tom, 2009, Volcanoes of the world; An illustrated catalog of Holocene volcanoes and their eruptions: Smithsonian Institution Global Volcanism Program Digital Information Series GVP–3, available online at *http://www.volcano.si.edu/world/*, last accessed April 20, 2009.

Simkin, Tom, and Siebert, Lee, 1994, Volcanoes of the world (2d ed.): Tucson, Geoscience Press, 349 p. (Superseded by Siebert and Simkin, 2009.)

Simkin, Tom, and Siebert, Lee, 2000, Earth's volcanoes and eruptions; An overview, *in* Sigurdsson, Haraldur, and others, eds., Encyclopedia of volcanoes: San Diego, Academic Press, p. 249–261.

Wicks, C.W., Jr., Dzurisin, Daniel, Ingebritsen, Steven, Thatcher, Wayne, Lu, Zhong, and Iverson, Justin, 2002, Magmatic activity beneath the quiescent Three Sisters volcanic center, central Oregon Cascade Range, USA: Geophysical Research Letters, v. 29, no. 7, 1122, doi:10.1029/2001GL014205.

Yellowstone Volcano Observatory, 2006, Volcano and earthquake monitoring plan for the Yellowstone Volcano Observatory, 2006–2015: U.S. Geological Survey Scientific Investigations Report 2006–5276, 13 p., available online at *http://pubs.usgs.gov/sir/2006/5276/.*

Appendix 1.   Disclaimer for the Volcano-Monitoring Instrumentation Database

The text of this Open-File Report serves as the metadata for the Volcano-Monitoring Instrumentation Database of 31 December 2008, which is included in this report. The disclaimer for the database is below.

This database, identified as the Volcano-Monitoring Instrumentation Database (VMID), has been approved for release and publication by the Director of the U.S. Geological Survey (USGS). Although this database has been subjected to rigorous review and is substantially complete, the USGS reserves the right to revise the data pursuant to further analysis and review. Furthermore, it is released on condition that neither the USGS nor the United States Government may be held liable for any damages resulting from its authorized or unauthorized use.

Although these data have been processed successfully on a computer system at the USGS, no warranty expressed or implied is made regarding the display or utility of the data on any other system, or for general or scientific purposes, nor shall the act of distribution constitute any such warranty. The USGS shall not be held liable for improper or incorrect use of the data described and/or contained herein. Neither the U.S. Government, the Department of the Interior, nor the USGS, nor any of their employees, contractors, or subcontractors, make any warranty, express or implied, nor assume any legal liability or responsibility for the accuracy, completeness, or usefulness of any information, apparatus, product, or process disclosed, nor represent that its use would not infringe on privately owned rights.